Value

Shella Pittsinger, Shelly Current,
and
Sherry Garrison

Trilogy Christian Publishers
A Wholly Owned Subsidary of Trinity Broadcasting Network
2442 Michelle Drive
Tustin, CA 92780

For information, address Trilogy Christian Publishing
Rights Department, 2442 Michelle Drive, Tustin, Ca 92780.
Trilogy Christian Publishing/ TBN and colophon are trademarks of Trinity Broadcasting Network.

For information about special discounts for bulk purchases, please contact Trilogy Christian Publishing.

Manufactured in the United States of America

10 9 8 7 6 5 4 3 2 1

Library of Congress Cataloging-in-Publication Data is available.

ISBN 978-1-64773-786-3 (Print Book)
ISBN 978-1-64773-787-0 (ebook)

Holy Spirit,
There are no words to articulate how You have impacted our lives. Thank You for always being present through every peak and every valley, ensuring our way. You are kind, loving, and so faithful. We honor You, Holy Spirit, and may our lives be an example of Your goodness to all who come before us. Thank You for bringing us together, being in the midst, and giving us the words to complete this book.

With the utmost love, we dedicate this book to our parents:
Harlan Murl Reid
Emila Margaret McKee-Genova

Thank you for your loving support and for being constant role models in and through our lives. As parents, you were the sounding board of which ultimately became the foundation on which we stand, fashioning the women that we are today—secure and settled in God's love.

To our precious father who passed on
Father's Day, June 19, 2016:
Thank you for your unconditional love and the countless hours you generously gave of yourself. You allowed the word of God to flow as a wellspring of living water, leaving an eternal imprint upon our lives. You truly mirrored the heart of our Heavenly Father.

To our beautiful mother:
You have taught us by example the worth of family and the value of prayer. Thank you, mom, for your unwavering love, your kindness, and your gentle spirit. We are truly blessed and honored to have you in our lives.

Our story is a story of redemption. In essence, we found our value in knowing the true gospel of grace, which is the person of Christ. For most of our lives, we were operating through the fundamental structure of religion where legalism flowed. That mindset, unknowingly, was bypassing the finished work of Jesus and His free gift of righteousness.

For by grace are ye saved through faith;
and that not of yourselves:
it is the gift of God:
Not of works, lest any man should boast.

Ephesians 2: 8–9 (KJV)

Value

God's eternal love is beautiful! Its tapestry is intricately woven upon our hearts. God set the mark of a person's value, because we are of our Father created in His image, we are held in the highest esteem above all that is most precious in God's sight. We are eternally loved and cared for in His precious son, Christ Jesus. Who we set our gaze upon, being that He is the light mirroring our true reflection, the image of our Heavenly Father.

> For God so loved the world, that He gave His only begotten Son, that whosoever believeth in Him should not perish but have everlasting life. For God sent not His Son into the world to condemn the world; but that the world through Him might be saved.
> John 3:16–17 (KJV)

> For I am not ashamed of the gospel of Christ: for it is the power of God unto salvation to everyone that believeth; to the Jew first, and also to the Greek. For therein is the righteousness of God revealed from faith to faith: as it is written, the just shall live by faith.
> Romans 1:16–17 (KJV)

Therefore, since we are justified by faith, we have peace with God through our Lord Jesus Christ. Through Him we have obtained access to grace in which we stand, and we rejoice in our hope of sharing the glory of God. More than that, we rejoice in our sufferings, knowing that suffering produces endurance, and endurance produces character, and character produces hope, and hope does not disappoint us, because God's love has been poured into our hearts through the Holy Spirit which has been given to us.

While we were still helpless, at the right time, Christ died for the ungodly. Why, one will hardly die for a righteous man—though perhaps for a good man, one will dare even to die. But God shows His love for us in that while we are yet sinners, Christ died for us. Since, therefore, we are now justified by His blood, much more shall we be saved by Him from the wrath of God. For if while we were enemies, we were reconciled to God by the death of His Son, much more, now that we are reconciled, shall we be saved by His life. Not only so, but we also rejoice in God through our Lord Jesus Christ, through whom we have now received our reconciliation.

Therefore, as sin came into the world through one man and death through sin, and so death spread to all men because all men sinned—sin indeed was in the world before the law was given, but sin is not counted where there is no law. Yet, death reigned from

Adam to Moses, even over those whose sins were not like the transgression of Adam, who was a type of the one who was to come. But the free gift is not like the trespass. For if many died through one man's trespass, much more have the grace of God and the free gift in the grace of that man Jesus Christ abounded for many. And the free gift is not like the effect of that one man's sin. For the judgment following one trespass brought condemnation, but the free gift following many trespasses bring justification. If, because of one man's trespass, death reigned through that one man, much more will those who receive the abundance of grace and the free gift of righteousness reign in life through the one-man, Jesus Christ.

Then as one man's trespass led to condemnation for all men, so one man's act of righteousness leads to acquittal and life for all men. For as by one man disobedient many were made sinners, so by one man's obedience many will be made righteous. Law came in, to increase the trespass; but where sin increased, grace abounded all the more, so that, as sin reigned in death, grace also might reign through righteousness to eternal life through Jesus Christ our Lord.

Romans 5:1–21 (YRSV)

I have been crucified with Christ; it is no longer I who live, but Christ who lives in me; and the life I now live in the flesh I live by faith in the Son of God, who loved me and gave Himself for me.

Galatians 2:20 (YRSV)

Blessed be the God and father of our Lord Jesus Christ, who has blessed us in Christ with every spiritual blessing in the heavenly places, even as He chose us in Him before the foundations of the world, that we should be holy and blameless before Him. He destined us in love to be His sons through Jesus Christ, according to the purpose of His will, to the praise of His glorious grace which is freely bestowed on us in the Beloved.

In him, we have redemption through His blood, the forgiveness of our trespasses, according to the riches of His grace which He lavished upon us.

For as He made known to us in all wisdom and insight the mystery of His will, according to His purpose which He set forth in Christ as a plan for the fulness of time, to unite all things in Him, things in heaven and things on earth.

In Him, according to the purpose of Him who accomplishes all things, and according to the council of His will, we who first hoped in Christ have been destined and appointed to live for the praise of His glory. In Him you also, who have heard the word of truth, the gospel of your salvation, and have believed in Him, were sealed with the promised Holy Spirit, which is the guarantee of our inheritance until we acquire possession of it, to the praise of His glory.

Ephesians 1:3–14 (YRSV)

For He is our peace, who has made us both one, and has broken down the dividing wall of hostility, by abolishing in His flesh the law of commandments and ordinances, that He might create in Himself one new man in place of the two, so making peace, and might reconcile us both to God in one body through the cross, thereby bringing the hostility to an end. And He came and preached peace to you who were far off and peace to those who were near; for through Him we both have access in one Spirit to the Father. So, then you are no longer strangers and sojourners, but you are fellow citizens with the saints and members of the household of God, built upon the foundation of the apostles and prophets, Christ Jesus himself being the cornerstone, in whom the whole structure is joined together and grows into a holy temple in the Lord; in whom you also are built into it for a dwelling place of God in the Spirit.

Ephesians 2:14–22 (YRSV)

But what things were gain to me, those I counted loss for Christ. Yea doubtless, and I count all things but loss for the excellency of the knowledge of Christ Jesus my Lord: for whom I have suffered the loss of all things, and do count them but dung, that I may win Christ, and be found in Him, not having mine own righteousness, which is of the law, but that which is through the faith of Christ, the righteousness which is of God by faith: That I may know Him, and the power of His resurrection, and the fellowship of His sufferings, being made conformable unto His death; If by any means I might attain unto the resurrection of the dead. Not as though I had already attained, either were already perfect: but I follow after, if that I may apprehend that for which also, I am apprehended of Christ Jesus. Brethren, I count not myself to have apprehended: but this one thing I do, forgetting those things which are behind, and reaching forth unto those things which are before, I press toward the mark for the prize of the high calling of God in Christ Jesus.

Philippians 3:7–14 (KJV)

Psalms 139:13–18 Amplified Bible (AMP)

13
For You formed my innermost parts;
You knit me [together] in my mother's womb.

14
I will give thanks and praise to You, for I am fearfully and
wonderfully made;
Wonderful are Your works,
And my soul knows it very well.

15
My frame was not hidden from You,
When I was being formed in secret,
And intricately and skillfully formed [as if embroidered with
many colors] in the depths of the earth.

16
Your eyes have seen my unformed substance;
And in Your book were all written
The days that were appointed for me,
When as yet there was not one of them [even taking shape].

17
How precious also are Your thoughts to me, O God!
How vast is the sum of them!

18
If I could count them, they would outnumber the sand.
When I awake, I am still with You.

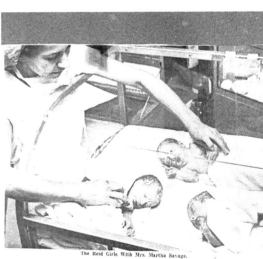

The Reid Girls With Mrs. Martha Savage.

Triplets Make Debut Saturday

By ALICE WRIGHT
Sentinel Staff Writer

Lacking the element of surprise, the birth of a set of triplets at Lincoln Park Hospital was accomplished smoothly Saturday between 1 and 2 p.m.

Barely an hour later, the father, Harlan Reid, 21, of 2817 Ronda Lee Road, Orchard Mesa, presented a happily relieved face to a reporter. No trace of nerves, no trembling hands, practically as good as new.

Somewhat less chipper, the 25-year-old mother, Emila, declined to have her picture taken, but was reserved pleased with the world in general.

Neither had yet seen the new arrivals, safely tucked away in incubators in the nursery. For triplets, they aren't so small: 3 pounds 2 ounces; 3 pounds 11 ounces, and 3 pounds 11 ounces.

The girls felt fine, and had no objections to a picture. They may as well get used to it — chances are many a camera will be aimed their way during the next few years.

The Reids have known for six weeks there would be three babies, so their only reaction was relief when all three turned up apparently normal and healthy.

Triplets are new in both parents' families, but on the Reid side there have been three sets of twins among their close relatives in two generations.

No special arrangements have been made at home for the new members of the family, as yet. "We wanted to see how things would turn out," Harlan said.

It's not a pressing matter anyway, since the babies will be kept in the incubators for quite a while, and the necessary preparations can be made after Mrs. Reid is released from the hospital.

Yes, it means buying cribs, diapers, clothing, everything a baby needs in triple supply.

Names have been discussed, but no decisions made. "That'll be up to her," said Harlan, with a nod toward the door of his wife's room.

One big family division was held up pending the babies' arrival: The matter of a new home.

"We want to build a house but we couldn't decide what we wanted until we knew how big a family we'd have, whether they were boys or girls," Reid said.

At home, four other children, 2 to 8 years old, await with interest the day when they can see their new sisters.

So do their grandparents, Mr. and Mrs. W. O. McKee of Fruita and Mr. and Mrs. Murl G. Reid of Palisade.

Reid works for his uncle, Howard Reid, a contractor.

Persuaded to sit quietly for a moment, Shella, Sherry and Shelly pose for their third birthday picture.
Sentinel Photo.

Reid Triplets, 3 Today, Unawed By Celebrity Status

By ALICE WRIGHT
Sentinel Staff Writer

The Reid triplets are three years old today.

Sherry, Shella, and Shelly are still unaware there's anything different a b o u t their status, and as yet don't realize they attract more attention than other youngsters.

In a household of seven children, there's not much reason to set the trio apart. And this is as it should be, their parents, Mr. and Mrs. Harlan Reid feel.

Since their second birthday, the Reids have come through a number of crises, the most trying of which was an episode of measles, when all seven came down at the same time.

Then one triplet had to have a cyst removed from her eye, another had pneumonia, and their four-year-old brother Randy, was burned and later developed pneumonia.

"We had somebody in the hospital every month during the summer," Mrs. Reid said.

Outwardly, the girls have changed little since last year —a little taller, a bit more hair, but so nearly the same size that clothes are interchangeable.

Speaking of clothes, t h e girls' preference for nudity appears to be past. Their mother learned to gauge their state of undress this summer by keeping an eye on the number of cars stopping in front

of the house to watch them at play.

Their feminine instincts are now taking over—they show a fondness for fluffy petticoats and barettes in their hair.

They know their names but t h e y call each other Sherry, since that's easies to say. Vocabularies are about normal for their age, the usual baby chatter.

They enjoy picture books singing the songs they learn at Sunday school, picnics, visiting relatives and all the normal activities of early childhood.

Their birthday celebration will be a cake served at tonight's family dinner—exactly the same as other family birthdays are celebrated.

Sherry, Shelly and Sheila Investigate The Contents Of Easter Baskets.

Easter Joy Threefold
With Triplets Around

By ALICE WRIGHT
Sentinel Staff Writer

Three little yellow-clad angels will appear at Sunday School this morning. Reports added their treble voices to the Easter chorus of the Assembly of God Church.

At four years old, the Reid triplets Shelly, Shelly and Sherry, have outgrown babyhood. They're quite conscious of the effect of crisp new dresses and grim hope of blond hair over each ear.

A fourth year of growing has added to their stature and accomplishments, but nothing in the way of differentiation. Their family, but few outsiders, know one from another. It's easy to speak to them by the wrong names, mistakes which the girls quickly correct.

Sheila is showing signs of independence, an inclination to wander off on her own pursuits and an attitude of maternal watchfulness over her sisters, according to their mother, Mrs. Marlan Reid.

Sherry and Shelly stick together like glue.

In size, appearance and disposition, the girls are utterly alike. They have the same sparkling brown eyes, the same mischievous smiles, the same cheerful familiar personalities, also the same number of teeth.

Other than a preference for different colors, they all dress the same things. Choosing between her own clothes for each day, Sheila selects yellow, Sherry blue, and Shelly pink.

They're quite like most 4-year-olds. They say inany color pictures, books, like stories, share toys, and chatter endlessly.

Last summer, their world expanded to encompass the vast outdoors. On weekend family outings, they learned to enjoy playing about the rocks on Grand Mesa, wandering under the shady trees, and eating picnic lunches beside the family camper.

Other exciting events since their last birthday were Halloween, Christmas, and visits to an Escalante Canyon ranch to visit their grandparents, Mr. and Mrs. Willard McKee.

They had their own ghost costumes for Halloween this year and enjoyed handing out the treats to visiting goblins.

For the first time, they were old enough to anticipate Christmas. Santa concentrated on housekeeping equipment, dishes, cupboards, clothing and cribs for their dolls.

The Reids are settled into a spacious home in Redlands Village now, big enough for the seven youngsters. The family just naturally divides itself, Mrs. Reid said — the two older girls, Karen, 13, and Debbie, 11, the two boys, Paul, 9, and Sandy, 4, and the "babies"

boys, although they're far from it now.

The girls are rarely seen away from home. Mrs. Reid has taken them shopping several times but after the crowds wore off, they became too much of a problem.

They take turns going to church with their grandmother, Mrs. Reid said. On Sunday mornings, but otherwise, they rarely congregate.

23

Redemption

Format to Redemption:

The greatest love story ever told

...the goodness of the Lord leads man to repentance.

Romans 2:4

In the foreknowledge of God—all things are

For by Him were all things created, that are in heaven, and that are in earth, visible and invisible, whether they be thrones, or dominions, or principalities, or powers: all things were created by Him, and for Him: And He is before all things and by Him all things consist.

Colossians 1:16–17

Nothing takes God off guard

Because He alone is, Jesus Christ the same yesterday, today and forever.

Hebrews 13:8

He is the Alpha and Omega, the beginning, and the end, which is, and which was, and which is to come.

Revelations 1:8

God's master plan to free man out from under the catastrophic demise of sin

Due to Adams disobedience to heed God's command (His word) in the Garden of Eden, Adam's transgression became the weight of sin that entered into the world and was passed down to all men, resulting in the fall of mankind.

> And the Lord God took the man and put him into the Garden of Eden to dress it and to keep it. And the Lord God commanded the man saying of every tree of the garden thou mayest freely eat. But of the tree of the knowledge of good and evil, thou shalt not eat of it: for in the day that thou eatest thereof thou shalt surely die.
>
> Genesis 2:15–16

> Wherefore as by one man sin entered into the world, and death by sin: and so death passed upon all men, for that all have sinned.
>
> Romans 5:12

What we may deem as loss, God sees as our gain. Adams disobedience ultimately became our gain in the reconciliation back to fellowship with our Heavenly Father, through one, Christ Jesus.

Man in need of a savior

Jesus is the light of the world. As the result of sin, the soul of man was eternally lost in a fallen state of darkness, without hope and in need of a savior. God in His loving kindness, gave freely His son Jesus, being the propitiation for the remission of sin.

> For all have sinned, and come short of the glory of God; Being justified freely by His grace through the redemption that is in Christ Jesus: Whom God hath set forth to be a propitiation through faith in His blood, to declare His righteousness for the remission of sins that are past, through the forbearance of God; To declare, I say, at this time His righteousness: that He might be just, and the justifier of Him which believeth in Jesus.
> Romans 3:23–26

The greatest love story ever told

> For God so loved the world, that He gave his only begotten Son, that whosoever believe in Him should not perish but have everlasting life.
> Johns 3:16 (KJV)

> For as by one man's disobedience many were made sinners, so by the obedience of one shall many be made righteous.
> Romans 5:19 (KJV)

THE FALL OF ADAM

God Gave A Specific Command in The Garden of Eden.

> The Lord God took the man and put him in the garden of Eden to till it and keep it. And the Lord God commanded the man saying, "you may freely eat of every tree of the garden: but of the tree of the knowledge of good and evil; you shall not eat for in the day that you eat of it you shall die."
>
> Genesis 2:15–17 (YRB)

Lucifer, being defiled unto himself with a heart of arrogance, became lifted up in his corrupt wisdom as God. Which was an act of sheer rebellion of utter defiance against God and His authority. Which resulted in his own downfall. The Word of God—

...I cast you to the ground.

Ezekiel 28:17

Spoken from God to Ezekiel:
In regard to the fallen angel Lucifer

You were the signet of perfection, full of wisdom and perfect in beauty. You were in Eden, the garden of God; every precious stone was your covering, carnelian, topaz, and jasper, chrysolite, beryl, and onyx, sapphire, carbuncle, and emerald; and wrought in gold were your settings and your engravings. On the day that you were created they were prepared. With an anointed guardian cherub, I placed you; you were on the holy mountain of God; in the midst of the stones of fire you walked.

You were blameless in your ways from the day you were created, till iniquity was found in you. In the abundance of your trade you were filled with violence, and you sinned; so I cast you as a profane thing from the mountain of God, and the guardian cherub drove you out from the midst of the stones of fire. Your heart was proud because of your beauty; you corrupted your wisdom for the sake of your splendor. I cast you to the ground.

Ezekiel 28: 12–17 (YRSV)

Garden of Eden

The iniquity that was found in Lucifer in Heaven was the same corrupt wisdom that he used against Eve, to entice her in eating of the tree of the knowledge of good and evil he said:

> "For God doth know that in the day ye eat thereof, then your eyes shall be opened, and ye shall be as gods, knowing good and evil."
>
> Genesis 3:5 (KJV)

> So, when the woman saw the tree was good for food, and that it was a delight to the eyes, and the tree was to be desired and to make one wise. She took of its fruit and ate; and she also gave some to her husband and he ate.
>
> Genesis 3:6 (YRB)

Self-advising an act of self-righteousness through one's own wisdom

Then the eyes of both were open, and they knew that they were naked; and they sewed fig leaves together and made themselves aprons.

Self/outward/five senses

Eating of the tree of the knowledge of good and evil being the sense ruled realm. Gathering all the information which is sifted through the carnal mind. Then forming a

33

judgement based out of a false truth. Which can vary according to circumstances.

Spirit/inward

Eating the tree of life, the inward man is receiving its information from the Spirit of God.

The mind of Christ

And they heard the sound of the Lord God walking in the garden in the cool of the day, and the man and his wife hid themselves from the presence of the Lord God among the trees of the garden. But the Lord God called to the man, and said to him, "Where are you?" And he said,

> "I heard the sound of thee in the garden, and I was afraid, because I was naked; and I hid myself." He said, "Who told you that you were naked? Have you eaten of the tree of which I command you not to eat?" The man said, "The woman whom thou gavest to be with me. She gave me fruit of the tree, and I ate."
>
> Genesis 3:7–13 (YRB)

By God asking, "Who told you that you were naked?" God knew that Adam had been disobedient. Having partaken of the tree of knowledge of good and evil, he was experiencing the effect of sin. Death was now in his soul and was working through the carnal mind.

> Because the carnal mind is enmity against God: for it is not subject to the law of God, neither indeed can be.
>
> Romans 8:7 (KJV)

God knew they would suffer spiritual death when they ate of their own wisdom from the tree of the knowledge of good and evil. Having transgressed against His word, they would sin and fall away from their true identity. Cut off from Him, the tree of life, they would have to rely on their own self-preservation. No longer receiving of His authority to rule and govern their souls.

> ...And The Lord God commanded the man, saying, "You may freely eat of every tree of the garden; but of the tree of knowledge of good and evil you shall not eat, for in the day that you eat of it you shall die."
> Due to Adam's disobedience, he was no longer under God's covering. All authority was relinquished legally to Satan.
>
> Genesis 2:16–17 (YRB)

> Wherefore, as by one-man sin entered into the world, and death by sin; and so death passed upon all men, for that all have sinned.
>
> Romans 5:12 (KJV)

The last supper

Now the first day of the feast of unleavened bread the disciples came to Jesus, saying unto him, "Where wilt thou that we prepare for thee to eat the Passover?" And He said, "Go into the city to such a man, and say unto him, 'The Master saith, 'My time is at hand; I will keep the Passover at thy house with my disciples.'" And the disciples did as Jesus had appointed them; and they made ready the Passover. Now when the even was come, He sat down with the twelve. And as they did eat, he said, "Verily, I say unto you, that one of you shall betray me."

And they were exceeding sorrowful, and began every one of them to say unto him," Lord, is it I?" And He answered and said, "He that dippeth his hand with me in the dish, the same shall betray me. The Son of man goeth as it is written of him: but woe unto that man by whom the Son of man is betrayed! It had been good for that man if he had not been born." Then Judas, which betrayed Him, answered, and said, "Master, is it I?" He said unto him, "Thou hast said."

And as they were eating, Jesus took bread, and blessed it, and brake it, and gave it to the disciples, and said, "Take, eat; this is my body."

And He took the cup, and gave thanks, and gave it to them, saying, "Drink ye all of it;

For this is my blood of the new testament, which is shed for many for the remission of sins. But I say unto you, I will not drink henceforth of this fruit of the vine, until that day when I drink it new with you in my Father's kingdom." And when they had sung a hymn, they went out into the mount of Olives. Then saith Jesus unto them, "All, ye shall be offended because of Me this night: for it is written, I will smite the shepherd, and the sheep of the flock shall be scattered abroad. But after I am risen again, I will go before you into Galilee."

Matthew 26:17–32 (KJV)

Gethsemane

Then cometh Jesus with them unto a place called Gethsemane, and saith unto the disciples, "Sit ye here, while I go and pray yonder." And He took with him Peter and the two sons of Zebedee and began to be sorrowful and very heavy. Then saith He unto them, "My soul is exceeding sorrowful, even unto death: tarry ye here, and watch with me." And He went a little farther, and fell on His face, and prayed, saying, "O my Father, if it be possible, let this cup pass from Me: nevertheless not as I will, but as thou wilt."

And he cometh unto the disciples, and findeth them asleep, and saith unto Peter, "What, could ye not watch with me one hour? Watch and pray, that ye enter not into temptation: the spirit indeed is willing, but the flesh is weak."

He went away again the second time, and prayed, saying, "O my Father, if this cup may not pass away from me, except I drink it, thy will be done."

And He came and found them asleep again: for their eyes were heavy. And He left them, and went away again, and prayed the third time, saying the same words. Then cometh He to His disciples, and saith unto them, "Sleep on now, and take your rest: behold, the hour is at hand, and the Son of man is betrayed into the hands of sinners. Rise, let us be going: behold, he is at hand that doth betray me."

Matthew 26:36–46 (KJV)

Jesus's betrayal and trial

And while He yet spake, lo, Judas, one of the twelve, came, and with him a great multitude with swords and staves, from the chief priests and elders of the people. Now he that betrayed Him gave them a sign, saying, "Whomsoever I shall kiss, that same is He: hold Him fast." And forthwith he came to Jesus, and said, "Hail, master;" and kissed Him. And Jesus said unto him, "Friend, wherefore art thou come?" Then came they, and laid hands on Jesus and took Him.

And, behold, one of them which were with Jesus stretched out his hand, and drew his sword, and struck a servant of the high priest's, and smote off his ear. Then said Jesus unto him, "Put up again thy sword into his place: for all they that take the sword shall perish with the sword. Thinkest thou that I cannot now pray to my Father, and he shall presently give me more than twelve legions of angels? But how then shall the scriptures be fulfilled, that thus it must be?"

In that same hour said Jesus to the multitudes, "Are ye come out as against a thief with swords and staves for to take me? I sat daily with you teaching in the temple, and ye laid no hold on me." But all this was done, that the scriptures of the prophets might be fulfilled. Then all the disciples forsook him and fled. And they that had laid hold on Jesus led Him away to Caiaphas the high priest, where the scribes and the elders were assembled. But Peter followed Him afar off unto the high priest's palace, and went in, and sat with the servants, to see the end. Now the chief priests, and elders, and all the council, sought false witness against Jesus, to put Him to death;

But found none: yea, though many false witnesses came, yet found they none. At the last came two false witnesses, and said, "This fellow said, 'I am able to destroy the temple of God, and to build it in three days.'"

And the high priest arose, and said unto him, "Answerest thou nothing? What is it which these witness against thee?"

But Jesus held His peace, and the high priest answered and said unto Him, "I adjure thee by the living God, that thou tell us whether thou be the Christ, the Son of God."

Jesus saith unto him, "Thou hast said: 'nevertheless I say unto you, 'Hereafter shall ye see the Son of man sitting on the right hand of power and coming in the clouds of heaven.'" Then the high priest rent his clothes, saying, "He hath spoken blasphemy; what further need have we of witnesses? Behold, now ye have heard his blasphemy. What think ye?" They answered and said, "He is guilty of death." Then did they spit in His face, and buffeted Him; and others smote Him with the palms of their hands, saying, "Prophesy unto us, thou Christ; Who is he that smote Thee?"

Matthew 26:47–68 (KJV)

Jesus before Pilate

When the morning was come, all the chief priests and elders of the people took counsel against Jesus to put Him to death: And when they had bound Him, they led him away, and delivered Him to Pontius Pilate the governor. Then Judas, which had betrayed Him, when he saw that He was condemned, repented himself, and brought again the thirty pieces of silver to the chief priests and elders, Saying, "I have sinned in that I have betrayed the innocent blood." And they said, "What is that to us? See thou to that."

And he cast down the pieces of silver in the temple, and departed, and went and hanged himself. And the chief priests took the silver pieces, and said, "It is not lawful for to put them into the treasury, because it is the price of blood."

And they took counsel, and bought with them the potter's field, to bury strangers in.

Wherefore that field was called, The Field of Blood, unto this day. Then was fulfilled that which was spoken by Jeremy the prophet, saying, "And they took the thirty pieces of silver, the price of him that was valued, whom they of the children of Israel did value; And gave them for the potter's field, as the Lord appointed me."

And Jesus stood before the governor: and the governor asked Him, saying, "Art thou the King of the Jews?" And Jesus said unto him, "Thou sayest." And when He was accused of the chief priests and elders, He answered nothing. Then said Pilate unto him, "Hearest thou not how many things they witness against thee?" And He answered him to never a word; insomuch that the governor marveled greatly.

Now at that feast the governor was wont to release unto the people a prisoner, whom they would. And they had then a notable prisoner, called Barabbas. Therefore, when they were gathered together, Pilate said unto them, "Whom will ye that I release unto you? Barabbas, or Jesus which is called Christ?" For he knew that for envy they had delivered him. When he was set down on the judgment seat, his wife sent unto him, saying, "Have thou nothing to do with that just man: for I have suffered many things this day in a dream because of him." But the chief priests and elders persuaded the multitude that they should ask Barabbas and destroy Jesus. The governor answered and said unto them, "Whether of the twain will ye that I release unto you?" They said, "Barabbas."

Pilate saith unto them, "What shall I do then with Jesus which is called Christ?" They all say unto him, "Let him be crucified." And the governor said, "Why, what evil hath he done?" But they cried out the more, saying, "Let him be crucified." When Pilate saw that he could prevail nothing, but that rather a tumult was made, he took water, and washed his hands before the multitude, saying, "I am innocent of the blood of this just person: see ye to it." Then answered all the people, and said, "His blood be on us, and on our children." Then released he Barabbas unto them: and when he had scourged Jesus, he delivered Him to be crucified.

Jesus is crucified

Then the soldiers of the governor took Jesus into the common hall and gathered unto Him the whole band of soldiers. And they stripped Him and put on Him a scarlet robe. And when they had platted a crown of thorns, they put it upon His head, and a reed in his right hand: and they bowed the knee before him, and mocked him, saying, "Hail, King of the Jews!" And they spit upon Him, and took the reed, and smote Him on the head. And after that they had mocked Him, they took the robe off from Him, and put his own raiment on Him, and led him away to crucify Him.

And as they came out, they found a man of Cyrene, Simon by name: him they compelled to bear His cross. And when they were come unto a place called Golgotha, that is to say, a place of a skull, they gave him vinegar to drink mingled with gall: and when He had tasted thereof, he would not drink.

And they crucified Him, and parted His garments, casting lots: that it might be fulfilled which was spoken by the prophet, "They parted my garments among them, and upon my vesture did they cast lots." And sitting down they watched Him there; And set up over His head His accusation written, *This Is Jesus The King of The Jews*. Then were there two thieves crucified with Him, one on the right hand, and another on the left. And they that passed by reviled him, wagging their heads, and saying, "Thou that destroyest the temple, and buildest it in three days, save thyself. If thou be the Son of God, come down from the cross."

Likewise, also the chief priests mocking Him, with the scribes and elders, said, "He saved others; Himself He cannot save. If He be the King of Israel, let Him now come down from the cross, and we will believe Him. He trusted in God; let Him deliver Him now, if He will have Him: for He said, 'I am the Son of God.'"

The thieves also, which were crucified with Him, cast the same in His teeth. Now from the sixth hour there was darkness over all the land unto the ninth hour. And about the ninth hour Jesus cried with a loud voice, saying, "Eli, Eli, lama sabachthani?" That is to say, "My God, my God, why hast thou forsaken me?"

Some of them that stood there when they heard that, said, "This man calleth for Elias." And straightway one of them ran, and took a spunge, and filled it with vinegar, and put it on a reed, and gave him to drink. The rest said, "Let be, let us see whether Elias will come to save Him." Jesus, when He had cried again with a loud voice, yielded up the ghost.

And, behold, the veil of the temple was rent in twain from the top to the bottom; and the earth did quake, and the rocks rent.

Matthew 27:1–51 (KJV)

When Jesus therefore had received the vinegar, he said, "It is finished." and bowed his head and gave up the ghost.

John 19:30 (KJV)

Joseph takes Christ's body and wrapped in linen

When the even was come, there came a rich man of Arimathaea, named Joseph, who also himself was Jesus's disciple: He went to Pilate and begged the body of Jesus. Then Pilate commanded the body to be delivered. And when Joseph had taken the body, he wrapped it in a clean linen cloth, and laid it in his own new tomb, which he had hewn out in the rock: and he rolled a great stone to the door of the sepulcher and departed. And there was Mary Magdalene, and the other Mary, sitting over against the sepulcher. Now the next day, that followed the day of the preparation, the chief priests and Pharisees came together unto Pilate, saying, "Sir, we remember that that deceiver said, while He was yet alive, 'After three days I will rise again.'

Command therefore that the sepulcher be made sure until the third day, lest His disciples come by night, and steal Him away, and say unto the people, 'He is risen from the dead:' so the last error shall be worse than the first."

Pilate said unto them, "Ye have a watch: go your way, make it as sure as ye can." So, they went, and made the sepulcher sure, sealing the stone, and setting a watch.

Matthew 27:57–66 (KJV)

In the end of the Sabbath, as it began to dawn toward the first day of the week, came Mary Magdalene and the other Mary to see the sepulcher. And behold, there was a great earthquake: for the angel of the Lord descended from heaven and came and rolled back the stone from the door, and sat upon it. His countenance was like lightning, and His raiment white as snow: And for fear of Him the keepers did shake and became as dead men. And the angel answered and said unto the women, "Fear not ye: for I know that ye seek Jesus, which was crucified. He is not here: for He is risen, as he said. Come, see the place where the Lord lay."

Matthew 28:1–6 (KJV)

It is finished

Through Jesus's blood, we are forgiven and redeemed out from under the curse of Adam's sin. Jesus's blood being the atonement which freed man from the tree of the knowledge of good and evil and was the reconciliation back to Christ, the tree of life.

For as by one man's disobedience many were made sinners, so by the obedience of one shall many be made righteous.

Romans 5:19 (KJV)

By God's grace, we have the freedom to choose.

Surely, He hath borne our griefs, and carried our sorrows: yet we did esteem Him stricken, smitten of God, and afflicted. But He was wounded for our transgressions, He was bruised for our iniquities: the chastisement of our peace was upon Him; and with His stripes we are healed. All we like sheep have gone astray; we have turned everyone to his own way; and the Lord hath laid on Him the iniquity of us all.

Isaiah 53: 4–6 (KJV)

World of Grace

Jesus lovingly brought us home to the heart of Abba Father, back to our true reality, the world of Grace. Whereby through His blood, we have been given free access through Christ to come and go at will. We are free to partake of and enjoy the fullness of Zoe Life (God Life).

But as it is written: Eye hath not seen, nor ear heard, neither have entered into the heart of man, the things which God hath prepared for them that love Him.

I Corinthians 2:9 (KJV)

The Holy Spirit

The prayer of Jesus
Our Father which art in heaven, hallowed be Thy name.
Thy kingdom come, Thy will be done
in earth, as it is in heaven.
Matthew 6:9–10 (KJV)

The prayer of Jesus was answered through the giving of the Holy Spirit. Heaven's best is here, now in the Earth as it is in Heaven.

Every good and perfect gift is from above coming down from the Father of lights, with whom is no variablesness neither shadow of turning.
James 1:17 (KJV)

Just think, our Heavenly Father placed a beautifully wrapped gift within the hearts of His children. Through the death, burial, and resurrection of His son Jesus, we have been given a new life in Christ Jesus. The fullness of God's grace through the person of Christ, our righteousness. Abba Father has made a way for His children to come home, back into His presence by simply receiving the exceptional gift that He placed within them.

Verily, verily I say unto you, He that entereth not by the door into the sheepfold, but climbeth up some other way, the same is a thief and a robber.

But he that entereth in by the door is the shepherd of the sheep.

To him the porter openeth; and the sheep hear his voice; and he calleth his own sheep by name.

John 10: 1–3 (KJV)

Then said Jesus unto them again, "Verily, verily, I say unto you, I am the door of the sheep."

John 10: 7 (KJV)

I am the door: by me if any man enter in, he shall be saved, and shall go in and out, and find pasture.

The thief cometh not, but for to steal, and to kill, and to destroy: I am come that they might have life, and that they might have it more abundantly.

John 10: 9–10 (KJV)

Christ is the gateway home, the access to the extraordinary, the world of grace. Coming full circle, back to our origin, back to the source of life (God life). Where in Christ the possibilities are endless. Living life to its fullest potential as God intended. All that we are and ever hope to be is found alone in Christ Jesus. Living the life that Jesus's blood purchased and redeemed on our behalf through Christ Jesus.

> Nevertheless, I tell you the truth; it is expedient for you that I go away: for if I go not away, the Comforter will not come unto you; but if I depart, I will send Him unto you.
> John 16:7 (KJV)

What an honor and privilege to have been given the Spirit of the living God, in the person of the Holy Spirit. The evidence of Christ Jesus finished work at the cross. By which we have been sealed with the holy Spirit of promise.

> Paul, an apostle of Jesus Christ by the will of God, to the saints which are at Ephesus, and to the faithful in Christ Jesus: Grace be to you, and peace, from God our Father, and from the Lord Jesus Christ. Blessed be the God and Father of our Lord Jesus Christ, who hath blessed us with all spiritual blessings in heavenly places in Christ:
> According as He hath chosen us in Him before the foundation of the world, that we should be holy and without blame before Him in love.
> Having predestinated us unto the adoption of children by Jesus Christ to Himself, according to the good pleasure of His will.

To the praise of the glory of His grace, wherein He hath made us accepted in the beloved.

In whom we have redemption through his blood, the forgiveness of sins, according to the riches of his grace; Wherein He hath abounded toward us in all wisdom and prudence; Having made known unto us the mystery of His will, according to His good pleasure which He hath purposed in Himself:

That in the dispensation of the fulness of times He might gather together in one all things in Christ, both which are in heaven, and which are on earth; even in Him. In whom also we have obtained an inheritance, being predestinated according to the purpose of Him who worketh all things after the counsel of His own will:

That we should be to the praise of His glory, who first trusted in Christ. In whom ye also trusted, after that ye heard the word of truth, the gospel of your salvation: in whom also after that ye believed, ye were sealed with that holy Spirit of promise. Which is the earnest of our inheritance until the redemption of the purchased possession, unto the praise of His glory.

Wherefore I also, after I heard of your faith in the Lord Jesus, and love unto all the saints,

Cease not to give thanks for you, making mention of you in my prayers; That the God of our Lord Jesus Christ, the Father of

Glory, may give unto you the spirit of wisdom and revelation in the knowledge of Him: The eyes of your understanding being enlightened; that ye may know what is the hope of His calling, and what the riches of the glory of His inheritance in the saints,

And what is the exceeding greatness of His power to usward who believe, according to the working of His mighty power, which He wrought in Christ, when He raised him from the dead, and set Him at His own right hand in the heavenly places, Far above all principality, and power, and might, and dominion, and every name that is named, not only in this world, but also in that which is to come; And hath put all things under His feet, and gave him to be the head over all things to the church,

Which is His body, the fullness of Him that filleth all in all.

Ephesians 1: 1–23 (KJV)

The Spirit of Truth

Howbeit when He, the Spirit of truth, is come, He will guide you into all truth: for He shall not speak of Himself; but whatsoever He shall hear, that shall He speak: and He will shew you things to come.

He shall glorify me: for He shall receive of mine and shall shew it unto you.

All things that the Father hath are mine:
therefore, said I, that He shall take of mine,
and shall shew it unto you.

John 16:13–15 (KJV)

Because we are children of God, we have been given the Holy Spirit within the light, illuminating the darkness. He is our guarantee, the promises of God. It is to simply follow the inner voice, the spirit of truth. As He leads, we follow. The Holy Spirit is a clear precise word, the path of which God has set before us.

Within ourselves

Within ourselves, we don't have the capability to grasp the love of God, nor the ability to genuinely love ourselves as well as others. But, through God's grace we have been given the Spirit of the living God; the fullness of the Godhead in the person of the Holy Spirit, the embodiment of God's love. His love is here to minister His healing power and to bring life back to what is dead. As we begin to be a first partaker of the Holy Spirit, we are allowing His love to minister His life back into those areas of brokenness. For within ourselves, we are broken and cannot truly love. As we draw from God's love within, we are receiving the purest form, Agape. It is loving to ourselves and we are then the extension of God's love to others. His love is beyond ourselves and past another's flesh, to love one another as Jesus loved without pointing fingers or condemning.

Dear readers,

With all the uncertainties of life, it is so reassuring to know that I have an anchor that supports all. I have been so blessed to have known the Lord since I was a child. Mind you, it was more of a knowledge of God, and throughout the years has blossomed into a beautiful and loving relationship with Christ Jesus. There is no other way without Christ. He is my way, my truth, and my life. He alone unlocks the treasures of Heaven, God himself.

So with great vigor, I count not myself to have apprehended: but this one thing I do, forgetting those things which are behind, and reaching forth unto those things which are before, I press toward the mark for the prize of the high calling of God in Christ Jesus.

Philippians 3:13–14

I would encourage those who may be questioning life itself to look to the Lord.

Jesus himself said, "I am come that they might have life, and that they might have it more abundantly." (John 10:10, KJV) It is only through a personal relationship with Christ Jesus, that you are truly alive.

Follow that inner voice, I promise you will find your way.

Faithfully,
Shella

Greetings,

To everything there is a season, and a time to every purpose under the heaven: A time to be born, and a time to die; a time to plant, and a time to pluck up that which is planted; A time to kill, and a time to heal; a time to break down, and a time to build up; A time to weep, and a time to laugh; a time to mourn, and a time to dance; A time to cast away stones, and a time to gather stones together; a time to embrace, and a time to refrain from embracing; A time to get, and a time to lose; a time to keep, and a time to cast away; A time to rend, and a time to sew; a time to keep silence, and a time to speak; A time to love, and a time to hate; a time of war, and a time of peace.

Ecclesiastes 3:1–8 (KJV)

May blessings and smiles be yours,
Shelly

Hello readers,

There is something so wonderful about knowing that you can call upon the Lord at any time. I have found that it is okay to be at peace, better yet, happy when the circumstances of life are not as you would have chosen. One day, I heard a minister say, "It is okay to be happy in the middle of your situation." That really has changed my perspective. When it is all said and done, people or situations should not dictate one's happiness. The truth be known, we have but one life to live. Enjoy, be at rest knowing God is faithful to the end.

This is the day which the Lord hath made; we will rejoice and be glad in it.
Psalms 118: 24

Blessings,
Sherry

Nuggets

#1

    Our Heavenly Father strategically placed a beautiful master plan within the heart of every man. His plan, purpose, and destiny for our lives. Through His grace, He has given to us the Holy Spirit, who is purposefully executing the will of God on the behalf of the believers. Bringing forth all things to fruition that pertain to our lives. It is to be continually conscious of who we are in Christ because therein the plan of God is revealed. Subsequently, our belief system is the cause which governs the direction over our lives. Our thoughts will either bring us into God's master plan or defer the plan. We have been given the freedom to choose life or death.

> For they that are after the flesh do mind the things of the flesh; but they that are after the Spirit the things of the Spirit. For to be carnally minded is death; but to be spiritually minded is life and peace. Because the carnal mind is enmity against God: for it is not subject to the law of God, neither indeed can be.
>
> Romans 8:5–7

#2

Through Christ Jesus, we the believers have been given all authority to rule and reign over the soulish realm, the carnal mind. Over every word that wars against the Spirit of truth and every thought that exalts itself against God. These words are strong in power, actively working to define and project a false identity; keeping our eyes sealed from our true identity that is hidden in Christ. It is of the utmost importance to have our minds continually renewed, immersing our souls deep into God's word, and allowing His waters to bathe and cleanse away the debris. Where in His light, our true reflection is revealed.

> Nay, in all these things we are more than
> conquerors through him that loved us.
> Romans 8:37

#3

In each new day God gives of His tranquility, that is the quiet of our souls.

Close your eyes and enter into His presence. Let His peace encapsulate you and quiet all the noise.

> Peace I leave with you, my peace I give
> unto you: not as the world giveth, give I unto
> you. Let not your heart be troubled, neither
> let it be afraid.
> John 14:27 (KJV)

#4

As human beings, we have the tendency to take upon the cares of this world, whether that be of ourselves or others. It is as if we are wheelbarrows going to and fro, picking up the loads, and then emptying those cares directly into our souls. Then we question why we do not have peace of mind. God did not create man to carry the load, for the care belongs to Him. As we cast off the care, we are then receiving God's love into the situation. Keeping our minds in perfect peace.

> Casting all your care upon him; for He careth for you.
>
> 1 Peter 5:7

> Thou wilt keep Him in perfect peace, whose mind is stayed on thee: because He trusteth in thee.
>
> Isaiah 26:3

#5

As believers in Christ Jesus, it's important to know that we are truly spirit beings of God. We are His temple, the body of Christ. We are one spirit joined with Christ and placed within these earthen vessels. It is our spirit man who is yielded and gives place to the Holy Spirit within. Allowing Him to have free access in and through our lives, accomplishing God's will here on the Earth. There is no place for human logic or reasoning to come into play, as believers we have been given the privilege of receiving from the wellspring of eternal life. The pure and undefiled wisdom of God, which leads and guides our way, establishing the footsteps of the righteousness.

Jesus our example:

> Believest thou not that I am in the Father, and the Father in me? The words that I speak unto you I speak not of myself: but the Father that dwelleth in me, he doeth the works.
>
> John 14:10

#6

No one is free of trials or tribulations, but to those who believe, we have the assurance that we are not alone. Christ Jesus is the anchor within the storm.

> These things I have spoken unto you, that in me ye might have peace. In the world ye shall have tribulation: but be of good cheer; I have overcome the world.
>
> John 16:33

In each new day, there is much to celebrate! God's love is all around. Make sure you take opportunities to stop and breathe in God's goodness and enjoy the life of His bounty. Whether that be taking in the refreshing scent of the sweet spring air, feeling the warmth of the summer sun, hearing the fall breeze rustling through the autumn leaves, or being captivated by the beauty of a snow-capped mountain. All the seasons of life are ours to enjoy.

Hold close your beloved family, friends, and loved ones; cherish them always. Be conscious of your surroundings and be present in both the chaotic and calm moments in life. Savor the time that has been given, let it not pass by as if it were a movie put in fast forward (here and then gone). Hold on to each moment as if it were the last. May our lives be lived to the fullest; may we embrace each new day with optimism and love one another beyond measure. We pray that your life will forever be unfolding to reveal God's beauty and enteral love.

Beyond

For the Lord Himself shall descend from heaven with a shout, with the voice of the archangel, and with the trump of God: and the dead in Christ shall rise first: Then we which are alive and remain shall be caught up together with them in the clouds, to meet the Lord in the air: and so shall we ever be with the Lord.

1 Thessalonians 4:16–17

Every individual conceived, whether that be past, present or in the future, for certain will face the afterlife. There is no getting around the fact that we are spiritual beings and when we die our spirits will exit these mortal bodies and enter into eternity. Saved or lost. Either through death or by the coming of our Lord Jesus, every man will inevitably come face to face with their maker. No doubt there will be those who are quick to say, "this is but foolishness." But, what if it is not? Frankly, the time we have been given on Earth compared to eternity is but a vapor.

> Yet you do not know the least thing about what may happen in your life tomorrow. What is secure in your life? You are merely a vapor like a puff of smoke or a wisp of steam from a cooking pot that is visible for a little while and then vanishes into thin air.
>
> James 4:14 (AMP)

Yet, be encouraged our spirit man is eternal and lives on. If you have received Christ Jesus as your personal savior, there is nothing to fear. We are simply going from one family to the other. Jesus has given His promise.

> Let not your heart be troubled: ye believe in God, believe also in me. In my Father's house are many mansions: if it were not so, I would have told you. I go to prepare a place for you.
>
> John 14:1–2 (KJV)

> And if I go and prepare a place for you, I will come again, and receive you unto myself; that where I am, there ye may be also.
>
> John 14:3 (KJV)

Christ is the passage to heaven

At the cross, Jesus's blood was the atonement for sin, the fulfillment of redemption. He alone is the passage to Heaven, the gateway home. When we receive the free gift of salvation, we are receiving a personal invitation from Abba Father to come back into his presence—of home. Back into His arms of security, where all is well. But, if you choose to turn your heart away from God, your soul will be lost in a state of utter darkness, separated from the life of God for eternity.

Repentance—a change of mind

Christ Jesus is coming back for His bride, are you ready?

Then shall the kingdom of heaven be likened unto ten virgins, which took their lamps, and went forth to meet the bridegroom. And five of them were wise, and five were foolish. They that were foolish took their lamps, and took no oil with them: But the wise took oil in their vessels with their lamps. While the bridegroom tarried, they all slumbered and slept. And at midnight there was a cry made, "Behold, the bridegroom cometh; go ye out to meet him." Then all those virgins arose and trimmed their lamps. And the foolish said unto the wise, "Give us of your oil; for our lamps are gone out." But the wise answered, saying, "Not so; lest there be not enough for us and you: but go ye rather to them that sell, and buy for yourselves."

And while they went to buy, the bridegroom came; and they that were ready went in with him to the marriage: and the door was shut. Afterward came also the other virgins, saying, "Lord, Lord, open to us." But he answered and said, "Verily I say unto you, I know you not." Watch therefore, for ye know neither the day nor the hour wherein the Son of man cometh.

Matthew 25:1–13 (KJV)

The Lord is not slack concerning His promise, as some men count slackness; but is longsuffering to us-ward, not willing that any should perish, but that all should come to repentance.

2 Peter 3:9 (KJV)

Salvation prayer

God so loved the world, that He gave His only begotten Son, that whosoever believers in Him should not perish but have everlasting life.

John 3:16

We would like to take this opportunity to personally invite you into the family of God. Simply say the prayer below. God bless you and welcome home.

Heavenly Father, I believe in your son Jesus
and His finished work at the cross.
I receive through the blood of Jesus,
the forgiveness of my sins.
I ask you into my heart and receive
you as my Lord and Savior.
In Jesus name,
Amen.

He that overcometh, the same shall be clothed in white raiment; and I will not blot out his name out of the book of life, but I will confess His name before my Father, and before His angels.

Revelation 3:5 (KJV)

My beautiful bride

My beautiful bride listen as the heart
of your bridegroom speaks.
My precious bride, how I love you.
Oh, how I long for you to enter in, and be in my presence.
Come, be with me awhile.
As I quiet your fears and bring tranquility to your soul.
Fall deep into my arms of love and tender care.
As I remind you, truly how precious you are.
When you were afar off, lost in sin,
I came and rescued you.
I laid my life down on your behalf, as my blood
was the atonement which freed you.
Together, through my death, burial, and resurrection,
we were raised one spirit, from the grave.
My beautiful bride, majestically adored in my righteousness.
You are valued above all that is most precious in my sight.
Close your eyes, I am here.
I will never leave nor forsake you.
I am with you always, throughout eternity.
Your bridegroom,
Christ Jesus

But God, who is rich in mercy, for His great love wherewith He loved us, even when we were dead in sins, hath quickened us together with Christ, by grace ye are saved; And hath raised us up together, and made us sit together in heavenly places in Christ Jesus: That in the ages to come He might shew the exceeding riches of His grace in His kindness toward us through Christ Jesus. For by grace are ye saved through faith; and that not of yourselves: it is the gift of God: Not of works, lest any man should boast. For we are His workmanship, created in Christ Jesus unto good works, which God hath before ordained that we should walk in them.

Ephesians 2:4–10 (KJV)

Endnotes

God is the source of life, the very essence of one's value. God wants to touch our hearts to show us how valued we are in His sight.

Since thou wast precious in my sight.
Isaiah 43:4 (KJV)

How precious also are your thoughts to
me, O God! How vast is the sum of them!
Psalm 139:17 (KJV)

Scriptures on Value

1 Timothy 4:8   Jeremiah 29:11

Psalms 139:14   Luke 12:7

1 Peter 1:18–19   Psalms 100:3

Genesis 1:26–27   Job 28:13

Matthew 6:26   John 15:13

About the Authors

Shella, Shelly, and Sherry were born and raised in the beautiful state of Colorado. They grew up in a close-knit family of eight children total. Together, they have raised nine amazing children who consider themselves more as brothers and sisters rather than cousins. The triplets have always had a heart for the Lord! They are extremely excited by where they are in this particular season of their lives and look forward to what lies ahead in their futures.

As close sisters, the triplets enjoy spending time in the mountains, traveling, and with family.

Acknowledgments

The Daily Sentinel of Grand Junction, Colorado
Jennifer Bridge Photography